KIDS
meet the

TRACTORS AND TRUCKS

by Andra Serlin Abramson and Paula Kovacs Ross

APPLESAUCE

Kids Meet the Tractors and Trucks

13-Digit ISBN: 978-1-60433-326-8
10-Digit ISBN: 1-60433-326-X

This book may be ordered by mail from the publisher.
Please include $2.50 for postage and handling. Please support your local bookseller first!

Books published by Cider Mill Press Book Publishers are available at special discounts
for bulk purchases in the United States by corporations, institutions, and other organizations.
For more information, please contact the publisher.

Applesauce Press Book Publishers
"Where good books are ready for press"
12 Port Farm Road
Kennebunkport, Maine 04046
Visit us on the web!
www.cidermillpress.com

Concept creator: Paul Beatrice
Cover design by Alicia Freile, Tango Media
Interior design by Gwen Galeone, Tango Media
All images courtesy of Shutterstock, unless specifically noted.
Typography: VAG Rounded
Printed in China

1 2 3 4 5 6 7 8 9 0

Dedicated to Meredith and Anna,
who might not know a lot about tractors
but who definitely know the sound of
an ice cream truck when they hear it.
-ASA

And for Anna's little brother Alex,
who has more truck books than
should be allowed, but none quite like
this one, which he proudly helped write.
-PKR

TABLE OF CONTENTS

INTRODUCTION

Vroom, vroom.

If the sight or sound of a big truck headed down the highway or a tractor working out in the fields makes you long to get behind the wheel and learn more, then please come along for the ride as we introduce you to 42 of the toughest, roughest, most hard-working trucks and tractors you'll find anywhere. From big semis to small bulldozers, diggers to cranes, balers to plows, this is your chance to get to know your favorite trucks and tractors on an up close and personal level. Want to know which truck can carry the most freight? Need to find out how long the longest road train was? Just want to learn more about haymakers and cultivators? Well, you've come to the right place because it's time for all you kids to meet the tractors and trucks!

AMBULANCE

Hey kids, it's me, your favorite **emergency** vehicle.

How do I know I'm your favorite?

Well, if you were in an emergency, wouldn't you want to see me speeding to your rescue? When you think of an ambulance, you probably think of a larger van or pickup type truck with flashing lights and screaming sirens, but actually, an ambulance is any vehicle used for transporting sick or injured people to, from, or between places of treatment.

The word ambulance comes from the Latin word *ambulare,* which means "to walk or move about" and the word originally meant a moving hospital that followed an army. It was during the American Civil War that vehicles for moving the wounded off the field of battle were called ambulance wagons.

There are a bunch of different types of us ambulances. The most common is the patient transport ambulance (sometimes called an ambulette). The second most common type

Type of Vehicle: Truck   **Wheels or Tracks:** Wheels

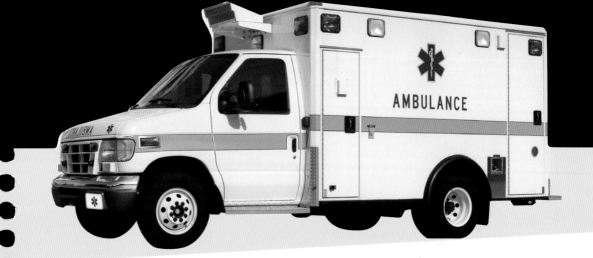

of ambulance is an emergency ambulance like me, which provide care to patients who need it immediately.

Emergency ambulances carry a lot of equipment. Some of the equipment I carry in my many compartments and holding areas includes a two-way radio, which allows my crew to pass information to doctors located at the hospital and get instructions back, lighting, mobile data terminals, and, of course, stretchers, bandages, and other medical supplies.

I've got to head out now. To be honest, I hope I never see you again, since if I do it's likely to be in an emergency situation. But if you do need me, rest assured, my crew and I will be there.

FUN FACT

Ambulances were first used to transport civilians during the 1830s. Advances in technology throughout the 19th and 20th centuries led to the modern **self-powered ambulances.**

AUTO TRAILER

Hi there, friends. I am an auto trailer and my job is to haul cars and small trucks around.

In some ways, I am very similar to a semi-tractor trailer truck because I have the same type of tractor cab on my front. However, instead of attaching a trailer full of stuff to my backside, my driver attaches an auto trailer that looks like scaffolding to hold vehicles.

The auto trailer connects to my tractor using a device called a King Pin, which my driver can easily remove to switch out the trailer for something else the next time he takes a trip.

I often take a load of cars from the factory where they are built to the dealership where they are sold. This keeps the cars from gaining any mileage from having to drive on the road. It also keeps the cars as shiny and new as possible for the new owner. No dents and scratches happen on my watch! But taking cars to the dealership is not the only

Type of Vehicle: Truck   **Wheels or Tracks:** Wheels

job I do. Sometimes I take cars that can no longer be driven from impound lots or from service stations to the junkyard.

I can typically carry 6-10 cars. There are weight restrictions on most of the roads, so I carry fewer SUVs at a time than smaller sedans. It takes a little bit of work to get all the cars settled in their correct place or unsettled and on the ground again. If you ever have a chance to watch me being loaded or unloaded, you should take it. I'm sure you'd find it as fascinating as I do. It's been great telling you about myself. Let's do it again soon!

FUN FACT

If you ever want to haul just one car from one place to another without putting any mileage on it, you can rent a **small auto trailer** that attaches to the back of a small truck or SUV and gets pulled like any other type of trailer.

BACKHOE

Hello, I'm a backhoe! Hey, that rhymes, isn't that funny?

I am also called a rear actor or back actor, and even a digger, but since those names don't rhyme, let's just stick with backhoe. I am a type of excavating machine and I am often found on construction sites or other places where big holes or trenches need to be dug or large amounts of stone or concrete need to be scooped up from the ground. I'm proud to say I am considered one of the most important machines on a building site.

I am called a backhoe because of the way my shovel scoops. Instead of pushing dirt or rubble forward, I dig by pulling the earth backwards.

I have three main parts. There's the cab where my driver sits, a two-part articulated arm, and the attachment at the end of the arm. As I mentioned, my arm has two parts. The first part is the one closest to the driver's cab, and it is called the boom. The section

Type of Vehicle: Excavator **Wheels or Tracks:** Either

which carries the bucket is known as the dipper or dipper stick. These two parts must work together in order to do the many jobs backhoes are called upon to perform.

As you've probably already noticed, I have tracks instead of wheels. My tracks are called crawlers and they allow me to move easily over rough or hilly ground. My tracks also help keep me steady, and because they help distribute my weight, they keep me from sinking into soft ground. That's not to say all backhoes have tracks. In fact, I have cousins with wheels (8 of them usually) that allow them to drive from one construction site to another. Well, it was sure nice meeting you. Be sure to come by the construction site and see me again sometime.

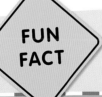

FUN FACT

The backhoe's scoop often has a metal bar called a "thumb" that grips against the scoop just like a person's thumb to help pick up objects.

BALER

Hi there kids. Have you ever wondered how farmers make those **giant cylinders** of hay that you see sitting around the field?

They use me! I'm a baler and I'm a very important attachment to a farm tractor! It's my job to make sure that all the hay that gets cut down when the farmer plows his fields can be dried and wrapped up to transport away.

My family of equipment can actually make two shapes of baled hay – cylinders and rectangles. The cylinder balers, like me, are more common, though. I roll up the hay inside my belly and then wrap twine or a net around it. Then, I open up a trap door and let the packaged hay roll out. Sometimes, my farmer will then wrap the hay bale in plastic to keep it dry. The hay bale will look like a gigantic marshmallow when he wraps it!

Type of Vehicle: Tractor **Wheels or Tracks:** Wheels

The hay bales that I make can weigh up to a ton, and sometimes even more! My farmer moves them around very carefully with a different type of equipment attached to my tractor called a bale spear. The bale spear is like a big stick that goes through the middle of the bale to lift it up and carry it around the farm.

Next time you are out in the country, try to find a farm that has hay bales in the field and count how many **giant marshmallows** you see!

FUN FACT

Balers can also be used away from the farm. A common use is at **recycling facilities** to package plastics and paper to be carried away.

BALLAST TRACTOR

Nice to meet you kids. I am a ballast tractor and it is my job to push or pull **really heavy** or **extremely large** loads.

Did you guess that I'm really strong? I have to be to move such big things. Not to get too complicated, but in order to get something so large to move, I have to be stronger than a force called "inertia." Inertia is the tendency of an object to resist any change in its motion. In other words, I need a really big engine to get my large loads to start moving.

Besides my strong engine, I need to be very heavy. My extra weight increases the friction between my tires and the surface of the road. Without my extra weight, called ballast, my wheels would rotate without generating any forward motion, kind of like what happens when your car's tires get stuck in the mud or snow.

Type of Vehicle: Truck

Wheels or Tracks: Wheels

I am designed to pull or push loads from a device called a drawbar. The drawbar transmits a horizontal force to the load. A strong chassis is required to support the extra weight of the ballast plus the pulling forces imposed by the drawbar. A reinforced chassis also allows multiple tractors to be attached together to increase my total power and traction.

A ballast tractor like me is often too heavy for regular roads so our use is a bit limited. However, when you need something really heavy pulled, you can always count on us ballast tractors.

See you **soon.**

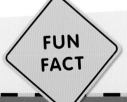

FUN FACT

The term **ballast** is derived from the nautical term describing heavy material added to a vessel to improve stability. For a ballast tractor, ballast is added over the driving wheels.

BEACH CLEANER

Do you like going to the beach?

Nothing says summer like a day of building sand castles and lying in the sun. If you've enjoyed these activities on beaches with clean sand, the kind that's soft and smooth and free of debris, then you should give me a big thumbs up. I am a beach cleaner and it's my job to remove anything from the sand that shouldn't be there.

One common place to find me is in seaside cities, where I drive up and down miles and miles of beach in order to provide the best experience for all the people who visit each day. I collect sand by way of a scoop or drag mechanism and then rake or sift anything large enough to be considered foreign matter, including sticks, stones, and trash. Besides natural beaches I am also useful for cleaning lake beaches, playing fields used for beach volleyball, and even playground sand pits.

My raking technology can be used on either wet or dry sand. To do this, I use a

Type of Vehicle: Tractor **Wheels or Tracks:** Either

rotating conveyor belt that has hundreds of tines (similar to the teeth in combs), to sift through the sand and remove surface and buried debris while leaving the sand on the beach. My raking machines can remove materials ranging in size from small pebbles to large pieces of driftwood. Since I'm not actually picking up any sand (which is pretty heavy) and am only lifting the debris, I can travel at a fairly high rate of speed, allowing me to cover a lot of ground each time I go out.

Ready to hit the beach? Remember, you have me to thank for the nice, soft sand you find there.

FUN FACT

In addition to their regular litter-removing uses, beach and sand cleaners have been used to clean up after **natural disasters**.

BUCKET TRUCK

Hey there, friends.

I am a bucket truck, also known as a **cherry picker,** a boom lift, basket crane, or hydraladder, and just like my many names, I have many uses. But before we get to my many uses you should know that I am a type of aerial work platform consisting of a platform or bucket attached to the end of a hydraulic lifting system. I am often mounted on the back of a large vehicle such as a truck (which is why I am called a bucket truck, naturally). My bucket is designed for a person to stand in and work from so it needs to stay still and steady. Except when it is moving, of course. Speaking of moving, the bucket (and the arm it is attached to) can be controlled either from the truck park or from a second set of controls located in the bucket itself. This means that the driver of the truck and the person in the bucket can actually be the same person. Cool, huh?

And now back to my uses. As you've already heard, I am often called a cherry

Type of Vehicle: Truck   **Wheels or Tracks:** Wheels

picker. That's because I was originally designed for use in orchards, where I made it a lot easier for workers to harvest fruit (not just cherries either). I am also used to service telephone, cable, and electrical equipment, put up Christmas lights and banners, and for painting the exteriors of large buildings. Some fire trucks have a cherry picker, which is known as a snorkel, instead of a ladder, and some window cleaners also use them. And I bet you didn't know that cherry pickers are also used in the mining and construction industries. It's been great telling you all about bucket trucks and cherry pickers, and whatever you call us, I hope you'll think of us often. Bye.

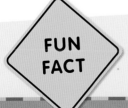

FUN FACT

Bucket Trucks have also been used in many forms of entertainment. For example, singer **Michael Jackson** would generally begin live performances of his song **"Beat It"** on a moving cherry picker.

BULLDOZER

Watch out! I'm coming through – and **nothing** gets in my way! I'm a bulldozer and my job is to **clear a path.**

While you might think of me as a giant construction truck, I'm actually a tractor with three very important pieces of equipment.

First, I have really wide tracked wheels, which is what makes me a tractor. I'm super heavy and my tracked wheels spread my weight around so I don't sink into mud or soft dirt. (Wouldn't that be embarrassing?!) Second, I have an enormous plate on the front of me called a blade. With my blade, I can push huge piles of soil, bricks, brush, or other construction site materials around without a problem. The bottom edge of my blade can be really sharp, so watch out. I use that sharp blade to cut through things – like tree stumps or tough roots. Third, I have a claw on my backside called a ripper. I use the ripper to loosen up hard clay, rocks, building debris,

Type of Vehicle: Tractor **Wheels or Tracks:** Tracks

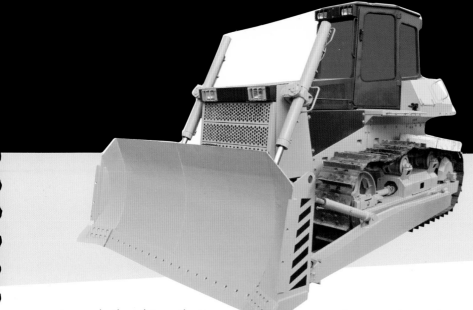

concrete, and other things that are hard to break through.

I can also make the ground surface level to carve out roads or prepare the site to build. There are some lighter members of my family used to remove snow from streets or to make snowy hills into skiing and snowboarding areas.

I'm very strong, too, mostly because I'm so heavy. I can push and pull things that other trucks can't.

In fact, some bulldozers in my family can tow **up to 70 tons!** So long!

FUN FACT

Very small members of the bulldozer family are called **calfdozers.**

BUS

OK, I know what you're thinking, and technically, you're right. I'm not really a truck. But give a vehicle a break.

I mean, it's not like they are going to make a whole book about buses, so when I heard about this book, I begged to get in. Luckily for both of us, the authors agreed. So here I am, a double decker bus, at your service.

The first thing you should know about buses is that we come in a bunch of different forms. There are school buses, commuter buses, minibuses, articulated buses, and of course, ones like me: a double decker. Our job is to transport people from one place to another as safely and quickly as possible, but also, in the case of public transportation, to make it easier for people to get around city centers and suburban areas.

Most buses like me run on diesel engines, but they didn't start out that way. The very first buses were created in the 1820s and

Type of Vehicle: Bus **Wheels or Tracks:** Wheels

were pulled by horses. Steam powered buses followed in the 1830s and electric buses came about in the 1880s. The first internal combustion engines in buses came about in the last years of the 1890s, and this is still the most common way to power us.

Buses were initially configured with an engine in the front and an entrance at the rear but now it is common to find buses with mid or rear-engine designs, with a single door at the front, or multiple doors throughout to help people get on and off more quickly.

But back to me, I have two separate floors so I can hold more people. I am a common sight in London and a few other cities where I often serve as special tour buses that allow people to see the sights without having to walk too far. Thanks for letting me have my say. Cheers!

FUN FACT

Some buses are equipped with **'kneel' air suspension** and have electrically or hydraulically extended under-floor ramps to provide level access for wheelchair users and people with baby carriages.

CEMENT MIXER

Hi Kids! Check me out!

I'm a Cement Mixer!

I am different than lots of construction trucks because I don't wait to get to work to do my job; I have a job to do even while I'm driving to work. I carry an enormous drum on my back that mixes cement, sand, and water to make concrete for sidewalks, building foundations, and other construction projects. My drum has blades inside that rotate constantly while concrete is inside, and the drum around the blades rotates too. By the time I get to work, the concrete is usually mixed and ready to go!

Concrete is heavy, so most of the time I drive right up to the construction site to drop off the mixed concrete. If I can't get all the way to the site, then I can attach a chute or conveyor belt to the back of my drum to help drop the concrete into the right place.

My heavy loads require lots of axles and tires for me to get around smoothly. My smaller brothers can get by with just the

Type of Vehicle: Truck **Wheels or Tracks:** Wheels

normal two axles, but some members of my family have four, five, or even six axles!

The nice thing about my work is that I typically don't have a very long day! Construction workers usually want my concrete in place quickly after I mix it up, so I can't travel that far! After a couple of hours, my concrete won't be good to use anymore. One thing I worry about is breaking down on the road, especially if I have a load of concrete mixing in the drum. If I break down, the drum stops turning and the concrete will get hard. If that happens, jackhammers or even dynamite need to be used to clean me out. Eeek!

It's been nice meeting you.

See you soon!

FUN FACT

My drum is usually made of steel, but I'm so heavy that recently workers have started building my drum from fiberglass!

COMBINE

Howdy, kids!

Do you want to be a farmer one day? If so, I'll be your best friend! I can certainly make your jobs on the farm much easier. I combine – get it? combine! – lots of harvesting jobs into one machine. Some people might say that I am really just a giant tractor that helps harvest different kinds of crops – usually the grain crops like wheat, rye, and barley – but really, I am more amazing than you'd think. Let me tell you a bit about what I do.

First, I grab the crops from their bottom with a series of rotating blades on my front and pull the crops into my belly. Next, I separate the grain from the straw that grows like a stem around the grain. Third, I save the grain in a container in my belly, and let the straw fall out of my back door. Later, a farmer will come by with a different tractor to deal with the straw that I leave on the ground.

Back in the old days, all of my jobs were done by hand. Can you believe it? It took a huge number of workers and an unimaginable number of hours to get all of

Type of Vehicle: Tractor   **Wheels or Tracks:** Wheels

my chores completed. In the 1800s, my great-granddaddy, a combine pulled by a horse was invented, and by 1911, my ancestors could move on their own.

I have different blades on my front that can be switched out depending on which type of crop I am going to work with. The piece I use to harvest corn is different, for example, than what I would use to harvest grain.

I don't mind working in all kinds of weather: heat, cold, rain, dry, whenever the farmer is ready to work, so am I. I even have special tires that keep me from sinking into the mud during a wet harvest time. Speaking of work, it's time for me to get back to it. See you soon.

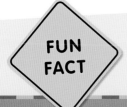

FUN FACT

The part of a combine that lets the straw out of the back door is called a **"straw walker."**

CRANE

I'm the most muscular truck in the land and I am proud to be able to help build everything from a house to a bridge.

That's because I carry a crane on my back all the time! I'm a truck-mounted crane and can be seen on many construction sites!

Cranes are really awesome tools that lift incredibly heavy things that people can't lift alone. Sometimes we lift large items straight up, or sometimes side to side (like lifting freight off of a boat or train). Either way, don't try this at home kids. It's a job for a crane like me!

I'm especially useful because I can travel on regular roads and highways. Many other cranes need special equipment just to get to the construction site, or they need to be taken apart to get to work, and then put back together after arriving at the site.

I can also move around while I'm carrying a load, while some other cranes have to stay

Type of Vehicle: Truck

Wheels or Tracks: Either

put. When I have to move a load from one place on the construction site to another, I need to move very slowly – probably slower than you ride your bike. I have to be careful that the load doesn't move too far side to side or I might tip over. That would cause a huge mess at the construction site and it would be dangerous too. I sure don't want anyone to get hurt. Thanks a lot for visiting with me.

So long!

FUN FACT

Depending on how many axles I have, I can lift almost 2,000 tons!

Hello friends!

I have a cool job on the farm

because I get to work in the fields

as the crops are growing!

I am a cultivator and I help the farmers reduce weeds in the crop beds. I have a frame with lots of spiky teeth on it that help me poke the ground. I'm usually attached to a small tractor and use my teeth to poke the soil and drag out weeds.

Sometimes, farmers use me in the fields after my friend the plow has prepared the soil, but before the crops have been planted. I'm really good at making sure the weeds are gone, and making sure the seeds will have a nice, soft bed of soil to lay in and grow.

The difference between me and the plow is that I can't dig as deep, but I can

Type of Vehicle: Tractor   **Wheels or Tracks:** Wheels

be used in smaller rows and for smaller areas that the plow is too big to get to. That's why I'm so useful for getting the weeds out from around the growing crops – I know not to disturb the actual plants!

Next time you visit a **farm**, see if you can see me in the **field** – I'm used all season long!

DUMP TRUCK

Wow! I just dumped a two-ton load of bricks.

I am proud to be a dump truck, one of the most popular and helpful trucks in the construction industry! I usually carry construction materials like dirt, sand, gravel, or bricks to or from a building site. I make a construction worker's job easier by dropping the materials where they are needed, so the workers don't have to haul them very far by hand.

I have a cool mechanical system on my back that lifts up one end of my truck bed, allowing the materials to slide out the other end. I need to be really careful that I'm on level ground when I let the materials slide out, otherwise I can tip over from the shift in weight.

I have cousins that do similar jobs but look a little different. Some of them dump their loads from the bottom or from the side,

Type of Vehicle: Truck   **Wheels or Tracks:** Wheels

and some are mounted on semi-trailers to carry a heavier load. I also have some really big cousins called haul trucks that stay inside construction sites all the time. They don't travel on regular roads like I do.

In the winter, my parts can be adapted to carry and spread salt and sand on icy roads.

And sometimes, I can even carry a plow on the front of my cab to clear snow and ice. As you can tell, I'm very versatile. I hope you've enjoyed learning a bit about me.

Have a **good** day.

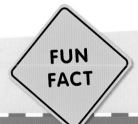

FUN FACT

The largest member of the standard dump truck family is nicknamed a *"centipede"* and has seven axles!

EXCAVATOR

Watch out kids, I'm moving mountains here!

I am called an excavator and I can move mounds of earth bigger than a car!

I have lots of parts to make me **strong** and **useful.**

My cab is called a house. I have a boom connected to the house, a stick connected to my boom, and a bucket connected to my stick! Got all that? It may sound complicated, but it's really pretty easy when you look at me.

I am used for lots of jobs around a construction site. I can dig foundations or trenches.

I can **demolish buildings.**

I can even **dredge rivers.**

Type of Vehicle: Excavator   Wheels or Tracks: Either

If I replace my bucket with a giant claw called a grapple, I can also lift really heavy pipes and move other equipment around the construction site. In fact, I like to accessorize and often change out my bucket into tools that are used for crushing, cutting, lifting, or boring holes. I also have different kinds of buckets that are good for moving through hard rocks.

Thanks for hanging with me.

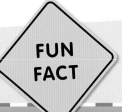

FUN FACT

In the United Kingdom, wheeled excavators are sometimes called **rubber ducks.**

FLATBED TRUCK

Quick, name 3 things that are flat.

Let's see, there's the floor, the world (just kidding), and me, a flatbed truck. It doesn't take a genius to figure out that I'm called a flatbed truck because my back is flat. As the name suggests, I have an entirely flat, level 'bed' body with no sides or roof. This allows for quick and easy loading of goods, even goods that would have a difficult time fitting inside the closed body of a regular semi-tractor trailer. For example, I have been known to transport large pieces of construction equipment, other trucks, and even whole houses.

Flatbed trucks can be either reticulated or rigid. Rigid flatbeds usually carry smaller loads since it is a bit more difficult for them to make turns. One type of rigid flatbed that is common in many areas is the flatbed tow trucks that pick up disabled cars and take

Type of Vehicle: Truck

Wheels or Tracks: Wheels

them to garages or junk yards. Reticulated flatbeds can carry larger loads because we have pivot points that allow us to turn around corners without tipping over. Some of the biggest loads that have been carried by reticulated flatbed trucks are the Space Shuttle, houses (or parts of houses), and some of the biggest pieces of construction materials you've ever seen.

Whenever I am travelling on regular highways with a really large load, I have to travel with special escort vehicles whose job is to keep other vehicles out of my way. As you can imagine, the larger my load the slower I have to go to keep it steady and safe. It's back to work for me. I hope you have a fun time learning about trucks and tractors.

FUN FACT

In Britain, flatbed trucks are usually called **flatbed lorries,** since in British English, the term 'truck' most commonly relates to railway vehicles, with the word 'lorry' more commonly applied to road vehicles.

FORKLIFT

Welcome kids.

I'm a forklift, and in warehouses, distribution centers, and even retail stores all over the world I'm about as important as any piece of equipment out there. We forklifts are made to lift heavy items to or from hard to reach places. We can put whole pallets on high shelves or move large, heavy boxes from one place to another. No job is too big or small for us to accomplish with ease!

My great granddaddy, the original forklift, was born in the 1920s, and each generation has improved our abilities and expanded our family. Today there are lots of different types of forklifts, ranging from a powered pallet truck, to an electrically powered rider stacker truck, to high-end specialty forklifts designed to navigate very narrow aisles and reach heights up to 40 feet tall.

As a typical counterbalanced forklift, my basic components include: my frame, a counterweight attached to my rear so that

Type of Vehicle: Truck **Wheels or Tracks:** Wheels

I don't tip over, a cab with roof, a power source, a mast which does the actual work of raising or lowering my load, tilt cylinders, which are hydraulic cylinders that pivot when I'm engaging a load, a carriage, which is the part where the forks or other attachments are, well, attached, and the load back rest that prevents the load from moving backwards when the carriage is lifted to its full height. All these pieces work together to help me do my job to the best of my ability.

I hope I answered all your questions about forklifts. TTYL.

FUN FACT

In a typical warehouse setting, most forklifts have load capacities of between **one to five tons.**

GARBAGE TRUCK

Watch out!

I'm coming through and I'm ready to **gobble up** your garbage!

As a garbage truck, I feast on all the trash from your neighborhood and take it to waste treatment centers to be sorted and treated, and then taken to a landfill.

My ancestors had open tops, but people quickly learned how to stop trash from falling out and how to stop the yucky smells by putting a top on the truck. Over time, our family has added mechanical parts that compact all of your trash inside the truck as we collect it, so we can fit more inside.

I like to be social and can be found in most towns.

It's hard for me to hide because I'm so noisy and big! Most of the time, a trash collector rides along the back with me to push the

Type of Vehicle: Truck   **Wheels or Tracks:** Wheels

trash inside of my bin. Garbage trucks that collect trash from big dumpsters don't need a person to help get the trash in the truck at all! In those kinds of garbage trucks, the driver uses controls to move special arms on the truck that lift the dumpster up and over the top, flipping out all of the trash. I'm very proud that I can keep your home and street neat and clean, and that I can take away all the stinky trash for you!

See you soon!

FUN FACT

I have different names in other parts of the world. I've sometimes been called a **"bin wagon"** or a **"bin lorry."** City departments will call me by my official name – **a refuse collection vehicle.**

HAYMAKER

Welcome to

my farm kids! You don't see me on every farm – only those farms that **grow lots of hay!** I am called a haymaker.

It is my job to mow the hay and then get it ready to dry out. Farmers call drying out hay "conditioning" it, so I'm also called a mower-conditioner, or a MoCo.

Here's how I work: I mow the hay in the field by cutting it down close to the soil. I use a sharp disc close to the ground like a lawn mower or a long sharp stick to chop it down. Then, I feed it through my two rollers that squish it flat and make it easier to dry out. I can sometimes shake it around too, in order to remove the waxy coating that grows

Type of Vehicle: Tractor **Wheels or Tracks:** Wheels

naturally on the hay. The first hay cut each season is particularly thick and takes a long time to dry, so flattening it out and shaking it around makes it dry out faster and more evenly.

Can you do me a favor? Pick up some **hay** on your local **farm** and think of me. Ta Ta.

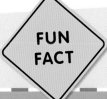

FUN FACT

Mowers and conditioners used to be separate pieces of farm equipment. Combining them into one tractor, a **MoCo,** was a huge improvement in farming, and the first MoCo was brand-named a **"Haybine."**

HUMVEE

Yo, what's up?

I'm a **High Mobility Multipurpose Wheeled Vehicle,** but you can call me by my nickname: Humvee.

You won't usually find me hanging out in your neighborhood, even in construction zones.

Instead, I'm a military vehicle, used by the United States military to help protect soldiers, move supplies, and climb to places most other vehicles would never be able to reach. While all the branches of the US Military use my services, I am mostly known as an Army vehicle, probably because the Army has more than 100,000 of us Humvees in its service.

There are more than 17 different types of Humvees out there in the world. Some of us act as ambulances for wounded soldiers. Others are cargo or troop carriers, and a few lucky ones carry missiles and other weapons.

Type of Vehicle: Truck

Wheels or Tracks: Wheels

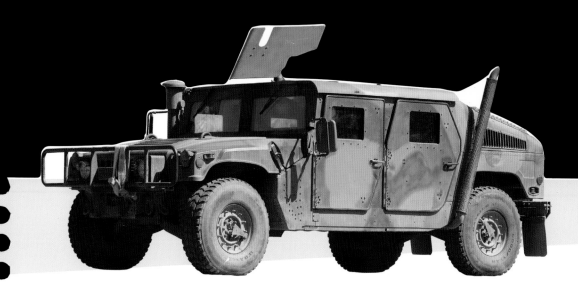

What's so great about me, you wonder? Well, I was specially designed to do hard jobs. I have 16 inches of ground clearance, which lets me move over big rocks and other debris without being damaged. As long as just one of my wheels is touching the ground I am able to move. I can also move through deep water. All Humvees can travel through 2.5 feet (.8 meters) of water, but some can also make it safely through more than 5 feet (1.5 m).

To protect us and our military crew, most Humvees are covered with tough armor that can really take a licking. It might get shot with machine gun bullets, hit with grenades, or even run over land mines and still keep the soldiers inside safe. Thanks for taking the time to find out more about me. As we say in the military, "dismissed!"

FUN FACT

The Army put three different prototypes of the Humvee through 450 tests before they chose the model built by **AM General.**

ICE CREAM TRUCK

Hey kids!

I bet I'm your very favorite type of truck. What am I? An ice cream truck, of course! During hot days I am the easiest and fastest way to get your favorite frozen treat. My job is to travel around from neighborhood to neighborhood, street to street, selling frozen desserts. You can usually hear me coming long before you see me since I play music to get the attention of kids in the neighborhood.

Wondering where the first ice cream trucks came from? The very first ice cream trucks hit the streets of Youngstown, Ohio in 1921 to celebrate a new invention: ice cream on a stick. The inventor of this frozen treat, Harry Burt, called his new delicacy "Good Humor Bars". To market his new product, Burt sent out a fleet of 12 chauffeur-driven trucks, all with bells to signal the truck's presence in the area.

Back in the 1920s, the technology to keep ice cream cold in the truck was pretty simple:

Type of Vehicle: Truck   **Wheels or Tracks:** Wheels

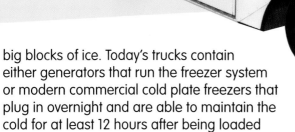

big blocks of ice. Today's trucks contain either generators that run the freezer system or modern commercial cold plate freezers that plug in overnight and are able to maintain the cold for at least 12 hours after being loaded onto the truck.

Ice cream trucks like me are common in the United States, Australia, New Zealand, the United Kingdom, and Scandinavia.

Places like Peru and Southeast Asia have ice cream motorcycles that travel around making people smile. Well, I hope I've made you smile a bit too.

Have a **great** day.

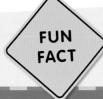

FUN FACT

Want to find out when an ice cream truck will be in your area? There's an app for that! Many local ice cream truck drivers display their routes or schedules on **social networking sites** so customers always know where and when to find them.

ICE RESURFACER

Good day to you kids. I am an ice resurfacer and it is my job to clean and smooth the surface of an ice sheet, usually at an ice rink.

The first ice resurfacer was developed by Frank Zamboni in 1949, which is why you often hear me referred to as a Zamboni machine. However, technically I should be referred to as an ice resurfacer and I would appreciate it if you called me by my actual name from now on.

Like most ice resurfacers, my insides are composed of 5 parts: a snow container, hot water tanks, a wash water tank, a conditioner, and a board brush. Most of my actual resurfacing components are contained in the "conditioner". Here's how I do it: I lower the conditioner to the ice surface, and use its weight to make the friction necessary for a large, sharp blade to shave off the top layer of ice. The ice shavings are then carried upward and sprayed into a large snow container.

Type of Vehicle: Ice Resurfacer

Wheels or Tracks: Wheels

Next, I use wash water to remove debris and snow from deep skate-blade cuts. To do this, I spray water onto the ice surface, loosening deep debris. A rubber squeegee at the rear of the conditioner allows a vacuum nozzle to pick up the extra water which is then filtered through a screen and recirculated. Finally, a layer of hot water is laid down to fill in the remaining grooves in the ice. I use hot water because it slightly melts the layer of ice below it, forming a stronger bond when frozen.

Think of me the next time

you are at the **ice rink!**

FUN FACT

A special machine called an **ice edger** is used to shave down the edges of the ice surface that the ice resurfacer cannot reach.

LADDER TRUCK

Greetings to you children.

You've probably seen me racing through the streets on the way to a fire or other emergency. That's right, I'm a type of fire truck, a ladder truck to be more exact. Here's something you should know right off the bat: I'm a type of fire truck, not a fire engine. The difference is that a fire engine carries its own water supply, while fire trucks like me carry a whole range of firefighting equipment and emergency gear.

If you live on a high floor of an apartment building and a fire breaks out, a ladder truck like me is what you'd want to see racing to your rescue. When I arrive at the scene of a fire, firefighters position me so that my ladder can reach to the tallest part of the building. Then the firefighters extend my "outriggers." These are special supports that come out from my sides to hold me steady when my ladder is in use. Without them, I might be in danger of tipping over. My longest ladder is called an "aerial ladder" and it can reach up to ten floors high, so

Type of Vehicle: Truck **Wheels or Tracks:** Wheels

you can see why some extra support might be needed.

The controls for my aerial ladder are located toward the back of my body. The ladder itself is attached to a turntable which means it is able to move 360 degrees. It only takes one firefighter to change the position or length of the ladder using my controls. If they had to do it by hand it would take six or even more people to get the ladder into place. I also have a bucket at the end of my ladder that provides a safe place for firefighters and the people they rescue to stand while the ladder is in motion.

Ooops, that's my **alarm bell.**

I'm outta here. Bye.

FUN FACT

A **tiller ladder,** also known as a hook-and-ladder, is a specialized turntable ladder mounted on a semi-trailer truck. It has separate steering wheels for front and rear wheels and requires two drivers.

LOADER

Hi there **kids.**

I'm a loader, a type of truck used mainly on building sites to scoop up large amounts of earth and rubble and load it onto other trucks to be taken away. I look a bit like my cousin, the bulldozer, but instead of pushing rubble along, my bucket is angled to pick it up.

Loaders like me usually have wheels instead of tracks. The wheels are much bigger than regular tires but they are small enough that we can drive on regular roads to get to our work site. Our wheels also help us move around the building site a lot faster than some bigger machines.

I have 3 main parts that help me do my job.

First there is a cab where my driver sits. He or she uses the controls in the cab to drive me to different locations and to raise and lower my bucket. The bucket is connected to the rest of me by the second main part of any loader: the boom. The boom is the part that actually

Type of Vehicle: Truck **Wheels or Tracks:** Either

goes up and down. Usually, hydraulics are used as the power source for the boom.

Finally, a bucket is connected to the boom. Buckets come in a few different sizes but they are usually wide and rectangular and have teeth along the edges to help me get a good grip on whatever I'm trying to pick up. But here's a cool thing about me: my bucket can be changed for another type of loading machinery, like a claw, that can pick up long pieces of wood, or a fork to lift heavy pallets or shipping containers. Pretty useful, huh? Well, I've got to get back to work now. My driver is calling me.

See you soon!

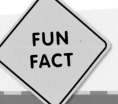

FUN FACT

The largest loader in the world is the LeTourneau L-2350. It has a bucket that could carry 88 tons in one scoop. That's the same weight as 13 elephants!

LOG LOADER

Did you ever wonder how wood gets from the **forests** to the **building site?**

Part of that trip is my job! I'm a log loader and it's up to me to make sure cut trees make it safely from the depths of the forests to the processing plant or store where they will be sold.

A long time ago, loggers would chop down a tree in the forest and roll it by hand onto a sled. The sled would be used to move the tree to a road. There it would be loaded onto a wagon or truck to be carried to a plant where it would be processed into a final product – like floorboards or paper. This was a really difficult job. The men had to be incredibly strong and work very hard for a long time just to get one log loaded onto the truck. Luckily, I came along and made life easier!

Type of Vehicle: Truck

Wheels or Tracks: Either

I have a couple of critical pieces of equipment for logging. First, I have a claw-like part on my front side that can grip a long log to keep it steady. Using the grips, I can move many logs into one stable pile. Then, I have a device underneath that looks like a forklift with two arms extending forward. I slide these arms under a stack of logs, lean back a little, and lift them up to load onto a truck. It's important that the logs don't fall off my arms while I'm moving around, so I have another arm that comes down on top to keep the logs in place. It's like giving the logs a great big bear hug. It's been nice meeting you all. Come back again sometime and say hello!

FUN FACT

The tool that loggers used before log loading trucks were invented is called a **peavy.** It was really just a long wooden stick with a strong iron hook on the bottom to grab the log.

MONSTER TRUCK

And now, straight from performances in arenas **big** and **small,**

it's time to meet me, a monster truck, one of the most athletic and highly decorated trucks you'll find anywhere. It's my job to do tricks, race, pull large objects, or even ride right over regular sized cars and trucks. Whatever makes you humans cheer the loudest.

Although my cab section isn't much different than a typical pick-up truck, my giant-sized wheels are so big I am not allowed on regular roads. That's why I do my performances in safe, controlled, atmospheres such as race tracks or arenas. Some monster trucks have wheels so large that a full grown adult could stand in the middle.

I am equipped with three separate remote shut-off switches that are designed to help prevent an accident if my driver loses control at any time. The first shut off switch is called the Remote Ignition Interruptor (RII), there is another one within the driver's reach in the cab, and another at the rear of the truck so that all electrical power may be shut

Type of Vehicle: Truck **Wheels or Tracks:** Wheels

off in the event of a rollover. As additional safety features, many monster trucks are shielded with a form of armor that protects our drivers from track debris and also allows for increased visibility.

But you are probably wondering, just how big are monster trucks? Well, one of my most famous cousins, named Bigfoot 5 is the tallest, widest, heaviest, pick-up truck in the whole world. His tires are 10 feet (3 meters) tall. Pretty impressive huh? Well, my next show is about to begin.

Thanks for taking the time to **visit** with me.

FUN FACT

Bigfoot 5's tires were originally used on an Alaskan land train that was used by the United States Army in the 1950s.

PAVER TRUCK

When your car has a **smooth ride** on the highway, it's because I've been there.

I'm a paver truck and I lay asphalt or concrete onto roads. You might even say I'm a smooth operator because of how hard I work to get the roads completely flat.

Here's how I make a road: first, my friend the dump truck feeds me asphalt that's already been mixed up and broken into tiny pieces. I have a conveyor belt inside that carries the asphalt under my cab to my backside, and then I let it drop onto the ground very slowly. Construction workers walk next to me to make sure the asphalt is spread around as I drop it. Two metal arms, one on each side, roll over the asphalt I have dropped to help control how deep of a layer it will be. Lastly, my friend the Roller Truck

Type of Vehicle: Truck **Wheels or Tracks:** Tracks

comes by to press the asphalt into the ground and smooth it out for an even surface.

When I pave really big roads, like Interstates and big bridges, sometimes I use concrete instead of asphalt. In those cases, I don't drop asphalt onto the road before I smooth it, and I don't use my arms. Instead,

a concrete truck drops piles of concrete in front of me and I push a long, straight piece of metal on my front called a screed over the piles to level it out. Next time you're driving around town, see if you can tell which roads are paved with asphalt and which ones might be paved with concrete! Bye.

FUN FACT

The first section of paved road was completed in 1891 in Bellefontaine, Ohio. Road builders hauled cement, gravel and sand to the worksite with wagons pulled by horses. The workers used shovels to mix it up and lay it on the ground. They even scored the surface to give the horses who would travel the road better footing.

PLANE TUG

If you're thinking, *"now there's a vehicle you don't see every day,"* boy, would you be right.

I'm a plane tug, also known as a pushback tractor. I am found only at the airport and even there I tend to keep a low profile (in more ways than one).

You see, it's my job to help push large aircraft away from the terminal after all the passengers have gotten on or off. Although most planes are able to move back from the gate on their own, the resulting jet blast or prop wash may cause damage to the terminal building or equipment. Engines close to the ground may also blow sand and debris forward and then suck it in to the engine, causing damage to the engine. Luckily, I'm here to avoid all this trouble.

In order to fit under the nose of the aircraft I am trying to tug, I need to use my low profile design. I also need to be really strong. Airplanes weight a lot! To help me get the traction I need, my body is built to be heavy

Type of Vehicle: Tractor

Wheels or Tracks: Wheels

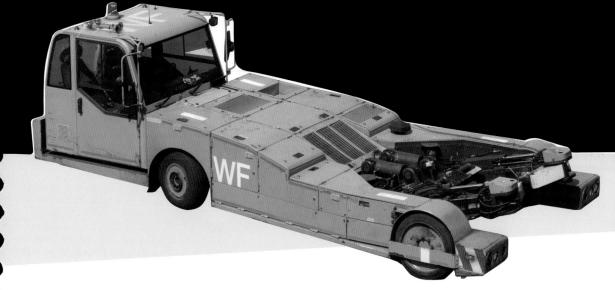

and sometimes extra weight, called ballast, is added to my frame. In fact, a typical plane tug meant to tow large aircraft can weigh up to 120,000 pounds (54 t).

There are two types of us pushback tractors: conventional and towbarless. Conventional tugs use a tow bar to connect the tug to the nose landing gear of the aircraft. Towbarless tractors do not use a towbar. Instead, they scoop up the nose wheel and lift it off the ground allowing the tug to maneuver the aircraft without anyone even having to be in the cockpit. Aw, do you have to go already? The next time you are at the airport, I hope you come back and visit me.

FUN FACT

Some airlines now suggest **towing aircraft** to the holding point of the runway with a plane tug in order to save on fuel costs and reduce environmental impact.

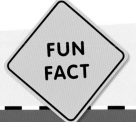

PLOW

Tractors on farms pull lots of different pieces of equipment. **One of those is me!** I'm a plow, and I have a few jobs in the fields on a farm. My first job is to turn over the soil.

I push weeds and old dried out crops underground and bring fresh dirt to the top. My second job is to aerate the soil. Aerate means to break up the top layer of soil to make it more loose, and allow air to get through it. My third job is to get the soil ready for planting the crops.

A long time ago, I was carried by horses or mules through the fields and the farmer had to push me up and down into the soil. Now, I'm attached to a tractor and I run with an engine. I have a big blade, and sometimes several blades, that reach into the soil and loosen it up. At the same time, I push the

Type of Vehicle: Tractor

Wheels or Tracks: Wheels

existing top layer with weeds and old crops down underneath a new top layer.

I am very critical to farming and help grow lots of kinds of food! What kind of farm food is your favorite?

Whatever it is, I hope you'll think of me, **the friendly plow**, the next time you eat it. **So long.**

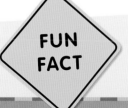

FUN FACT

Some farmers spell my name **plough** instead of plow. I answer either way.

RECREATIONAL VEHICLE

OK, be honest, is there any truck on the road as cool as me? I mean, who else is actually a travelling house complete with a kitchen, bathroom, bedroom, and living room. I am also referred to as a motorhome or camper, and within those categories there is a lot of variation as to the size of the vehicle and whether we are meant to be lived in full time or are just for a weekend out in the woods.

There are two different kinds of RVs. Some, like me, have their own motor and are driven from a steering wheel and other controls found in the front of the vehicle. In this type of motor home, people can do a lot of the same activities while the vehicle is moving that they can do in their own living room when they are at home. Watch TV? Check. Go to the bathroom? Check. Get a snack from the fridge? Check.

The other type of recreational vehicle is meant to be towed behind another car or truck, and while the vehicle is on the road, people don't usually stay inside. Instead they ride in the towing vehicle. It's safer that way.

Type of Vehicle: Truck   **Wheels or Tracks:** Wheels

If you ever have a chance to travel in a motorhome like me, I bet you would be impressed. There is actually a lot of room inside and the designers were very careful to find lots of nooks and crannies where my owners can easily store all their belongings. When we get to our destination, which is usually a special RV park or campground, we can be hooked up to water and power sources that allow us to run just like any regular house.

If you are ever thinking about seeing the world, I hope you'll take me along with you.

I **promise** I'll make the trip as much **fun** as the **destination!**

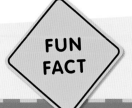

FUN FACT

You'll find **RVs** on the sets of many movies. Movie stars like to use them as dressing rooms, meeting spaces, and rest areas when they are on location.

RECYCLING TRUCK

Do you recycle? I do! I pick up the **newspapers, plastics, glass** and **metals** from your trash bins and take them to be made into new products.

I admit it – I look a lot like a garbage truck. We are a lot alike, but also very different. We collect completely different things! He collects trash (yuck!) and I collect stuff that can be made into wonderful, brand new, exciting things! We do work the same way, though. You put out your recyclables and I put them into my truck to be hauled away.

There are two types of trucks in my family. Some of us can haul away recyclables that are mixed together – this is called co-mingling or single stream recycling. Some of us require that your recyclables be separated into piles of glass, paper, aluminum and plastic – called multi-stream recycling. In this case, we have different chambers inside the truck to keep

Type of Vehicle: Truck **Wheels or Tracks:** Wheels

all of the recyclables separate or we use a different truck for each type of item. When you mix up your recyclables to be taken away, it's much easier for you, but tougher for us, because we then have to take everything to a sorting facility to be separated before we can

haul each type of item where it needs to go.

Thanks for listening and remember to **recycle!**

FUN FACT

If a community allows the recyclables to be mixed up and put at the curb, more people participate in **recycling** and more items are able to be accepted, than if the community requires people to sort their recyclables.

ROAD TRAIN

Hey there mates!

Have you ever seen a truck as long as me? I bet not! As you can tell, I'm practically as long as a railroad train, which is why I'm called (you guessed it!) a road train. Road trains like me are not usually found in busy cities or on busy highways. In fact, most places have restrictions against my kind that prevent me from operating in congested areas. I don't take it personally though. When you are as big as I am, safety comes first!

Since I can't operate in busy places, you would mostly find me in remote areas of Argentina, Australia, Mexico, the United States, and Canada. Like a regular train, my job is to move freight efficiently. My basic structure is a regular tractor unit that might pull a lot of different types of trailers, but as a "longer combination vehicle," I am able to pull two, three, or even more trailers or semi-trailers. I may also be called a "triple," "turnpike double," and "Rocky Mountain double."

As you might have suspected, it is rather difficult to drive a truck as long and heavy as

Type of Vehicle: Truck   **Wheels or Tracks:** Wheels

I am. Governments have rightly put in place speed and weight restrictions designed to keep my driver and other vehicles on the road with me safe.

Road trains vary in size from a "B-Double," (also called a "B-Train") to a "Powertrain" (also called a "Body and six"). The B-Double consists of a tractor towing a specialized lead trailer that has a fifth-wheel mounted on the rear towing another semi-trailer, resulting in two articulation points. The Powertrain can have up to six trailers. They operate at mines in the western Northern Territory of Australia.

Thanks for learning a bit about me and my road train cousins. Cheers!

FUN FACT

On February 18, 2006, an Australian built Mack truck with 112 semi-trailers pulled the load 328 feet (100 metres) to capture the record for the **longest road train** ever pulled with a single prime mover.

ROLLER TRUCK

Watch your toes, folks! **I'm comin' through** and I wouldn't want to flatten your feet!

Do I look a little familiar? You might have met my cousin the paver truck a little earlier. I am a roller truck and after the paver truck lays down the asphalt on a road, it's my job to pat down the asphalt and make sure it's as smooth as can be. My large round drum, which I wear on my front, rolls over everything in its path! I have to be really heavy to flatten the asphalt as much as possible, so my drum is made of a lot of heavy metal.

I can **flatten** out roads or dirt with just the weight of my **heavy drum,** but sometimes I can vibrate my drum to add **pressure** to the road or dirt.

Type of Vehicle: Truck **Wheels or Tracks:** Neither!

I'm not used only on roads, though. I also can be used at landfills to flatten the mounds of soil. However, when I work at a landfill, I don't wear a smooth drum like I do when I work on the roads. Instead, I wear a heavy round drum that has lots of little knobs coming out of it. This kind of drum just presses the ground down as much as possible, but does not make it smooth. I like the change of pace when I get to switch out my roller drums! Speaking of a change of pace, I need to get back to work. Have a good day.

FUN FACT

The first rollers were not trucks at all, but **big round drums** that were carried down a dirt road by horses to make the road flatter.

SEMI-TRACTOR TRAILER

I am the king of the road! As a semi-tractor trailer, it's my job to haul everything from groceries to clothing to toys from one place to another.

I pick things up on ports at the coastlines and sometimes I drive thousands of miles to deliver them to the stores right in your neighborhood. I'm a pretty large vehicle. I have to be to carry as much cargo as I do. Since I'm so much larger than all the regular cars on the road, my driver needs to have a very special driver's license called a CDL, or Commercial Driver's License, which requires extra training. This makes sure that he or she knows how to drive me safely in all types of weather and road conditions.

My cab is configured one of two ways. Either the engine is in front of where my driver sits, like in a regular car, or the engine is underneath the driver so that the driver can

Type of Vehicle: Truck **Wheels or Tracks:** Wheels

see a little easier down to the road in front of the truck. The trailer on the back is hitched to the tractor with a device called a king pin. The trailer overlaps the tractor so that the heavy weight of the filled trailer is carried in part by the cab.

The king pin is easily removed or adjusted so that the trailer can be switched out and the tractor can drive away to go pick up a different load.

Next time you drive on the highway, count how many of us you can see!

FUN FACT

Trailers come in all sizes and can even be frozen inside to haul frozen groceries to the stores.

SNOW PLOW

Well, the weather outside is frightful… for you maybe, **but not for me.**

I'm a tough snowplow. When snow starts falling, my phone starts ringing, and as soon as you can say snowblower, I'm on the job. There are a few different types of us snowplows and we are sometimes referred to as winter service vehicles.

Today, the most basic kind of snowplow is just a shovel attached to the front of a pick-up truck. That's good enough for clearing most driveways. For bigger jobs, you have to think bigger truck. You might see a snowplow attachment on the front of a bulldozer, garbage truck, or even a dump truck. However, when the job really needs to get done, you have to call in the big guns, like me, a dedicated snowplow machine. Instead of just a shovel, I use a specialized snowblower machine that works by churning up the snow with a spinning drum and then

Type of Vehicle: Truck **Wheels or Tracks:** Either

shooting it out to the side of the road in a big plume. It's pretty cool (get it? Cool!) to watch actually.

While the idea of pushing snow off the road seems pretty low-tech, I use some pretty high-tech methods to get the job done right. I use Global Positioning System (GPS) receivers, heads-up displays, and infrared cameras to see where I am going and to avoid obstacles. I also have a satellite navigation system connected to a weather forecast feed which allows my driver to choose the best areas to treat. My systems can even adapt to changing conditions, ensuring I provide the very best service possible. It was so cool meeting you. Let me know if any snow is coming your way, and I'll be there to take care of it.

FUN FACT

The very first snow plows were just horsedrawn **wedge-plows** made of wood.

STREET SWEEPER

Hi Kids! Have you ever helped your parents **clean the house** by running the vacuum cleaner?

I do the same thing, but I do it outside on the streets! I am a street sweeper, and I have been keeping neighborhood streets clean since the 1840s!

My ancestors were really just giant brooms connected to horses. They swept debris off the streets. More modern street sweepers work much more efficiently to collect small pieces of litter. Most of us street sweepers today have rotating discs to loosen and sweep up dirt and debris from a street, and then we can vacuum it into a container on the truck to be disposed of properly. We even spray water on the street while we're sweeping to help us loosen more dirt and also to prevent lots of dust from flying around.

Type of Vehicle: Truck

Wheels or Tracks: Wheels

We can be very useful for helping the environment because we can pick up little bits of trash that pollutes our local streams by getting into stormwater drains at the side of the road. Some of us street sweepers can even pick up particles of dust smaller than you can see, but which can be very damaging to local waterways! We're proud to help clean up the environment!

Stay green!

FUN FACT

The first modern street sweeper was purchased and used in Boise, Idaho in 1913! The technology improved in the 1970s to pick up smaller particles of dust that can pollute waterways.

SUCTION EXCAVATOR

Quick, suck in your breath. Did you feel the power of the air coming into your lungs?

Well, now you know a tiny bit about what I do. I'm called a suction excavator and I am a type of construction vehicle. My job is to remove earth or other materials from holes using suction, similar to how your household vacuum cleaner picks up the dirt that get in your carpets. Of course, I am way more powerful that any old vacuum cleaner. In fact, when I am turned up to my highest power setting I can suction up materials at a speed of 224 mph (100 meters/second).

The suction nozzle coming out of the main part of my body has two handles for people to hold on to it. That way they can aim it where it needs to be. The end of the tube has points on it that are used to cut up pieces of earth that are too big to fit through my tube. I also have a special grille over the opening of my tube which the workers holding the tube can use to stop the suction so that I am able

Type of Vehicle: Excavator **Wheels or Tracks:** Wheels

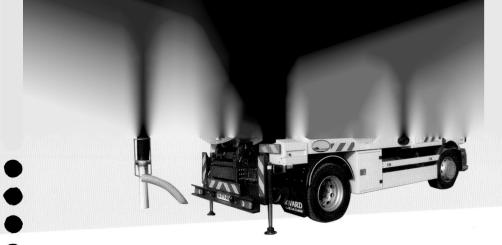

to drop things that may be too large for me to swallow.

One of my best uses on construction sites include safely locating underground utilities and removing earth from around them. This process is also referred to as "daylighting", since the underground utilities are exposed to daylight during the process.

I am proud to say I am much in demand these days. In fact, in many places I am considered the "best practice" for certain construction jobs and some places insist on my presence.

Speaking of being in demand, I'm ready to get back to work now. **See you soon.**

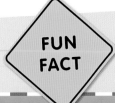

FUN FACT

Suction excavation techniques can be an effective way to locate, with virtually 100% accuracy, all underground structures in an excavation zone. **Vacuum excavation** is also typically more cost effective than hand digging.

TANKER

Well hello there children.

I am a tanker truck and when you see one of my kind heading up the highways you can be sure we are doing an important job. For example, we could be carrying liquid petroleum or oil. We might be moving gasoline from area refineries to your local gas station. If you see a tanker truck at the airport, it is probably carrying the fuel needed to gas up an airplane or two. And there is a refrigerated kind that carries perishable liquids like milk from dairy farms to processing or bottling plants.

Tanker trucks come in a wide range of sizes from kind of big to really, really large. In fact, tanker trucks are actually known by their size. Large trucks typically have volume capacities ranging from 5,500 to 9,000 gallons (21,000 to 34,000 L). Small tanker trucks generally have a volume capacity of less than 3,000 gallons (11,000 L).

Are you wondering what we are made of? Well, that depends on what we are meant to haul, but in general tanker trucks

Type of Vehicle: Truck

Wheels or Tracks: Wheels

are constructed of aluminum, carbon steel, stainless steel, and Fiberglass Reinforced Plastic (FRP).

Some pretty special tanker trucks are able to carry a few different types of liquids at a time. They do this by dividing the tank into compartments. A common use of compartmentalization is by gasoline

delivery trucks who use it to carry different grades of gasoline to service stations in just one trip.

Thanks for listening to me. It's been **my pleasure** meeting you.

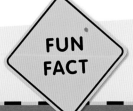

FUN FACT

Tanker trucks are difficult to drive because of their high center of gravity.

TOW TRUCK

Has your car ever broken down on the side of the road? If you answered yes, then **I probably helped you!**

I am a tow truck and it's my job to carry cars that aren't working to a service station. Sometimes I take cars that are parked illegally to the police station. And sometimes, like after a car accident, I might haul a car to the junkyard!

I have a flat steel bed in the back of my cab that my driver can tilt down toward the ground. After my driver backs up to a car that needs towing, he tilts the bed down and connects the car to the bed using a chain. Depending on which of my family members helps your car, the chain might connect to the car in one of a few different ways. The first way is hooking around the axle beneath the two front or rear wheels. The second way is

Type of Vehicle: Truck **Wheels or Tracks:** Wheels

to hook the chain to the frame of the vehicle under the bumper. The last way is to slide a piece of equipment called a wheel lift under the tires to lift it up. No matter which way the chain connects to the car, it's always attached to a winch on the truck that pulls in the chain in order to slide the car up onto the flatbed.

Oh, I hear a call coming in over my radio. It's time to go out and help another motorist. See you soon.

FUN FACT

The International Towing and Recovery Hall of Fame and Museum in **Chattanooga, Tennesee** displays tow trucks through the ages. The first tow truck was invented in the same town in 1916.

TRACTOR

Hiya kids.

I'm a tractor and you can go ahead and thank me now for helping farmers grow the yummy fruits and vegetables you like to eat. When I work on a farm, my job is to move slowly across the fields pulling a variety of implements that turn the soil, plant the seeds, or even create hay bales. As you can imagine, I have to be pretty strong to do all that.

The basic farm tractor has an open air cab with just a steering wheel and speed controls, but today's modern tractors often have enclosed cabs complete with heating and air conditioning and a variety of switches and buttons that are used to control the speed, gears, towing apparatus, and other functions. There are usually four or five foot pedals for my operator to use located on the floor of the cab. One pedal is the clutch, two pedals control the brakes, the fourth pedal is for the throttle, and the fifth is used to operate the rear differential lock (diff-lock), which prevents wheel slip. Almost every tractor

Type of Vehicle: Tractor

Wheels or Tracks: Usually wheels, occasionally tracks

today features a three-point linkage system. This hitch allows for easy attachment and detachment of implements while allowing the implement to function as a part of the tractor, almost as if it were permanently attached to it. This type of linkage has been successful in preventing me from turning over if the attachment I am towing hits an obstacle.

This is good news since unfortunately tractor-related injuries account for approximately 32% of the fatalities and 6% of the nonfatal injuries in agriculture and over 50% of those deaths are because of tractor overturns.

It's been great getting to know y'all. Think of me the next time you eat your broccoli. Yum, my favorite! Bye.

FUN FACT

The highest speed of most tractors is around 25 mph (40 km/h) but a few can go as fast as **50 mph** (80 km/h).

TUNNEL BORING MACHINE

Hi Kids, I'm a **tunnel boring** machine. You don't see me very often because most of the time I live underground making tunnels.

Maybe I'm not technically a truck, but I do come in many sizes, and I am often custom built to dig a particular tunnel.

The largest tunnel borers are over 62 feet (19 meters) wide! When tunnel borers are that big, we can't get to our construction site in one piece, so we are taken apart to get to work, and then put back together.

To dig a tunnel, I use a flat wheel on my front that leads me through the ground and fits like a puzzle piece inside the new tunnel. The wheel rotates while I push it through

Type of Vehicle: Machine

Wheels or Tracks: Either

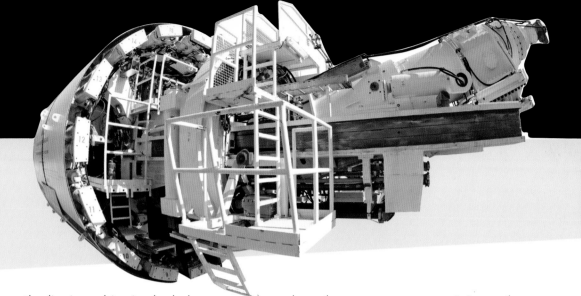

the earth, digging a big circular hole. The blades on my wheel are different depending on the type of ground I need to cut through. But no matter what, I leave a much smoother tunnel wall than other types of tunnel digging methods.

After I'm done digging the tunnel, I'm usually taken apart and sent back to a factory where they can reuse my parts in another custom built machine or recycle them into something else. I don't mind though.

I'm a **tunnel boring machine** and **digging** is my game. Bye.

FUN FACT

My nickname is **"mole"** because of the work I do underground.

Good afternoon. Looking to get wet?

Well, I may be able to help with that. As a water tender I have the ability to transport large amounts of water from wherever I can find it to the scene of a fire. I can use streams, lakes, hydrants, or regular pipes to pick up my water, then I store it in my tanks, and take it where it needs to go. Often I have to travel to out of the way places where hydrants or pipes don't exist, like forests, or rural areas.

While my pumps aren't as powerful as a regular fire engine, and I might not be able to provide enough power to the largest hoses, if there isn't a working fire hydrant in the area, I'm your truck. I can carry loads of up to 5000 gallons of water (19,000 liters), although carrying around 1000 gallons of water (approximately 3800 liters) is more common.

In place of water, some tenders also carry foaming agents and extinguishing powders or gases that are used in situations where water would not help put out the fire. In Australia, there are special water tenders

Type of Vehicle: Truck **Wheels or Tracks:** Either

that are actually converted semi-trailer fuel tankers, capable of holding many thousands of liters of petrol, foam, or other retardant. These are most often used in severe HazMat situations, such as oil refinery fires or fuel tanker accidents, where a large and continuous volume of whatever will put out the fire is needed ASAP.

It's been **great** telling you about me. **Have a nice day.**

FUN FACT

Water tenders are often used to help clean up after a **large flood** by using their power to pump water out of affected areas.

GLOSSARY A-H

Articulated Vehicle: a vehicle which has a pivoting joint in its construction, allowing the vehicle to turn more sharply.

- -

Axle: central shaft for a rotating wheel or gear.

- -

Ballast: heavy material added to a vehicle to improve stability.

- - - - - - - - - - - - - - - -

CDL: Commercial Drivers License.

- -

Counterweight: equivalent counterbalancing weight that balances a load.

- -

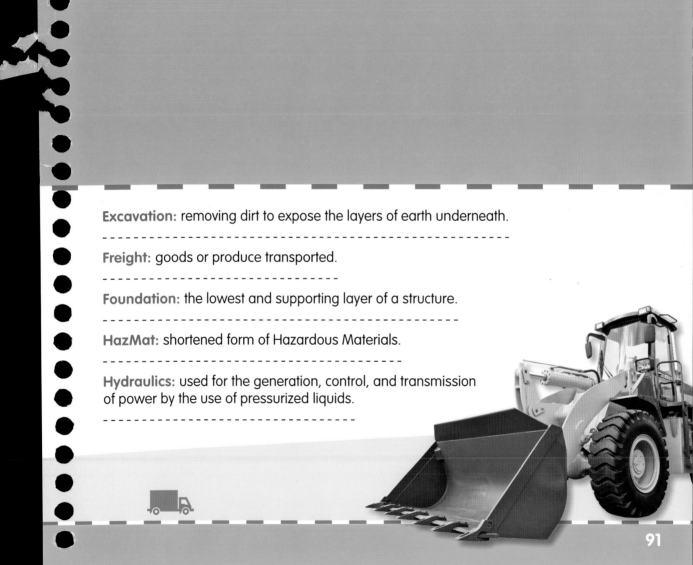

Excavation: removing dirt to expose the layers of earth underneath.

- -

Freight: goods or produce transported.

- -

Foundation: the lowest and supporting layer of a structure.

- -

HazMat: shortened form of Hazardous Materials.

- -

Hydraulics: used for the generation, control, and transmission of power by the use of pressurized liquids.

- -

GLOSSARY I-Z

Inertia: the tendency of an object to resist any change in its motion.

Petroleum: also known as crude oil, a naturally occurring flammable liquid consisting of a complex mixture of hydrocarbons and other liquid organic compounds that are found in geologic formations beneath the Earth's surface. Petroleum is recovered mostly through oil drilling.

Reticulation: resembling or forming a net or network.

RV: shortened form of Recreational Vehicle, also known as a motorhome.

Torque: the tendency of a force to rotate an object about a pivot. For example, pushing or pulling the handle of a wrench connected to a nut or bolt produces a torque (turning force) that loosens or tightens the nut or bolt.

Wheelspin: when the wheels on a vehicle turn but the vehicle doesn't go forward.

Winch: mechanical device that is used to pull in (wind up) or let out (wind out) or otherwise adjust the tension of a rope or cable.

PHOTO GALLERY

Ambulance
Rob Wilson

Auto Trailer
Vibrant Image Studio

Backhoe
Art Konovalov

Baler
Gordana Sermek / Shutterstock

Ballast Tractor
SRA Stan Parker / Wikipedia

Beach Cleaner
Naturespixel

Bucket Truck
Rob Wilson

Bulldozer
Art Konovalov

Bus
James Steidlszdv

Cement Mixer
Bram van Broekhoven

Combine
Vaclav Volrab

Crane
Skryl

Cultivator
DeshaCAM

Dump Truck
WitthayaP

Excavator
Photobac

Flatbed Truck
Robert Pernell

Forklift
Stephen Clarke

Garbage Truck
Rob Wilson

Hay Maker
Elridge

Humvee
StockPhotosLV

Ice Cream Truck
Paul Stringer / Shutterstock

Ice Resurfacer
Michael Klenetsky

Ladder Truck
artis777

Loader
Art Konovalov

Log Loader
Tund

Monster Truck
Natursports / Shutterstock

Paver Truck
Dmitry Kalinovsky

Plane Tug
Brendan Howard

Plow
Fotokostic

Recreational Vehicle
Condor 36

Recycling Truck
Johnny Habell

Road Train
Neale Cousland

Roller Truck
Dmitry Kalinovsky

Semi-Tractor Trailer
Rob Wilson

Snow Plow
Patrik Mezirka

Street Sweeper
Baloncici

Suction Excavator
Courtesy of Alamo

Tanker
Rihardzz

Tow Truck
Dmitry Vereshchagin

Tractor
Photobac

Tunnel Boring Machine
Fotokon / Shutterstock

Water Tender
Brad Sauter

About Applesauce Press

What kid doesn't love Applesauce!

G ood ideas ripen with time. From seed to harvest, Applesauce Press strives to craft books with beautiful designs, creative formats, and kid-friendly information on a variety of topics. Like our parent company, Cider Mill Press Book Publishers, our press bears fruit twice a year, publishing a new crop of titles each spring and fall.

"Where Good Books Are Ready for Press"

Visit us on the web at
www.cidermillpress.com
or write to us at
12 Port Farm Road
Kennebunkport, Maine 04046

Other titles in the KIDS MEET Series:

Kids Meet the Dinosaurs
Kids Meet the Presidents
Kids Meet the Snakes

Coming Soon:

Kids Meet the Bugs
Kids Meet the Reptiles